Bring Back the Fun

Activity Ideas for Caregivers and People with Dementia

By Marcie M. Jones

Co-Founder of Gentog, LLC

DEDICATION

I worked with seniors when I was a teenager and young adult. I loved it. We opened Gentog, and I was able to work with seniors again. I loved it. Then God decided I needed to learn first hand what it means to be a family caregiver…my Gram broke her shoulder and could no longer live alone. For two years she shared our home with my family, and I learned to live with someone with dementia. This book is dedicated to all of the seniors that I've met through the years…but especially to my Gram. She was always my "fun" Gram, so it's fitting that she taught me how to Bring Back the Fun…even with dementia.

CONTENTS

INTRODUCTION

For the past five years we have had the honor and fun of creating an Adult Day Program in Tigard, OR. When we started this venture, we cared for one person at a time. Five years later we routinely care for 25-30 seniors daily. Most of the people we care for have mild to moderate dementia.

It is our goal that the people who come to our center feel safe and loved. We aim to have fun every single day.

This journey with dementia can be daunting. But we've learned that it can also be lots of fun. The stories we hear, the laughs we share...we wouldn't trade this experience for the world. We've decided that it's time to share some of what we've learned so families facing life with dementia can know that there is still fun to be had. There are still lots of moments to enjoy. You may have to enjoy things differently than before...but different does not have to be sad.

This book is written as if your loved one is

speaking to you. A person with dementia may have difficulty expressing his/her feelings. Sometimes you have to guess what will be enjoyable...and that can change day to day...even moment to moment.

Read through the book, and find a couple of ideas that could work for you and your loved one. Give them a try. If one idea doesn't work, try something else. The time you have left is limited...you should find the fun in the moments, and cherish it.

We've included photos of our program so you can see the joy that we experience every day. We pray that you, too, can create some fun on your own family's journey with dementia.

LAUGH WITH ME

Yes, dementia has taken away some of my abilities....but if I used to love to tease and laugh, I probably still do. Don't be afraid of offending me. Keep joking. Keep teasing. Share a laugh with me.

If I don't understand the joke, I may still laugh, and I may still enjoy the moment. Simply being with you and sharing a smile or a laugh is enough to make me happy.

You may just be surprised. Sometimes I will say something that really does make sense and is funny! When that happens, laugh with me.

Sometimes I may not get the joke, and the moment won't go well. If I get upset, use the magic words "I am sorry", and re-set the moment. That's the beauty of this dementia journey…I enjoy (or don't enjoy) each moment as it comes. If you do something that doesn't sit right with me, I probably won't remember it. So keep trying!

Laugh with me, find humor every day, and enjoy the moments with me.

SING WITH ME

Did you know that the brain retains music until the end? It's one of the first things we respond to as babies, and one of the last things we lose as our brains fade. So let's share some music!

If you have a musical ability, share it with me. Sing for me (I'll likely join in). Play the piano for me. Enjoy making music, and I'll enjoy it right along with you, however I can.

Do you have a Karaoke machine? They make some Karaoke CDs with old-time favorites, hymns and patriotic songs. I'll enjoy those…be sure to get the ones with the background singers. I'll do much better singing along than trying to carry the song.

If you don't have musical ability, use the technology we have today, and create some musical times for me. Fill your iPod with songs we can enjoy together, and play them in the car when we drive somewhere. If I have always enjoyed country music, I still will today. I will definitely tap my toes and nod my head…I may even join in if I remember the song.

Create a playlist of patriotic songs. If I am a veteran (or if I lived through wartime), I will love to hear those familiar songs, and I will sing along.

Don't forget the religious hymns of my youth. Even if you do not know me as a religious person, you may be surprised to know that I will sing along with the old hymns. I likely shared them as a child with my parents or grandparents, and I will find joy and peace in them today. I may weep a little as I sing "Amazing Grace", but that doesn't mean you shouldn't play it. Weeping isn't bad, it's just an emotion. Share it with me.

Is it Christmas time? Play those holiday tunes for me. I love them, and I really do know those standards. I like to sing them.

If I sing beautifully, enjoy it. Remember when I used to sing to you or with you. Enjoy those memories with me. If I can't hold a tune, don't judge me…join me! Singing with you may improve my tone (or not)….but it will definitely make me happy!

If I am sad or lost today, softly sing a familiar song. I will probably join in. Or maybe I'll just lean in and relax a little. Either way, it will help.

If we're doing chores, add music that I'll enjoy. Singing together always makes things more fun. If we're exercising, add music. If we're sitting and knitting together, add soft music.

Sing with me. Sing joyfully. Sing loudly with me if that's what I do. Sway with the music and enjoy it with me. Music soothes the soul…mine and yours.

DANCE WITH ME

That's right! If I enjoy singing, I will probably enjoy dancing too.

If I don't walk well, our "dance" may simply be swaying in place. Or I may surprise you and do a turn or two. Hold my hand and sway to the music. I can dance from my chair. Waltz with me, if that's what we used to do. I may not remember every step, but I will enjoy being in your arms again.

Dance for me. Turn that music on, bring in the kids, and dance for me! I love to see the little ones enjoying the Hokey Pokey. I delight in seeing the teenagers do their crazy dancing. I will definitely enjoy watching a dancing show on TV with you.

Dancing is joyful. It's a physical expression of emotion. I may not be able to say what I think or feel anymore. But maybe, just maybe, I can still show you in dance. Even if my body doesn't move like it used to, you will surely see the emotion in my eyes as I dance the way I can today.

HELP ME CHERISH MY OLD FRIENDS

It's hard for me to be around my friends now. Maybe I don't know how to contact them anymore…who can remember all of those phone numbers and addresses? Or maybe I can't figure out the phone anymore. So help me call a dear friend.

Take me to visit my sister-in-law and best friend in the home where she lives. When you see us together, and our conversation doesn't make sense, don't worry. If we are peaceful or happy, that's all that really matters. We don't have to have deep conversations that you understand…we may simply enjoy being together.

If you know some of our history, help us remember the stories. Say "Remember when you two took that crazy road trip to Vegas?" Start the conversation, and we'll probably join in. You may have to carry the majority of the talking, but if we're nodding along, we're enjoying the story. Being together and sharing those memories is good for us. It may also be good for you, if you let it be. Don't fret about how it's so different now. Just help us enjoy being together again.

Writing letters may be hard for me now. But maybe I'd enjoy reaching out that way. Bring a card and ask who I'd like to send it to. Suggest a friend that might enjoy hearing from me. Help me write a short note (be my secretary and do the writing if I can't do that anymore). The person who receives the card will likely be happy to hear from me. If they write back, imagine my joy in receiving a letter! I may carry it in my purse and re-read it a dozen times a day...**and I'll enjoy it every single time**. Such value for so little time and effort!

HELP ME MAKE NEW FRIENDS

Yes, I can still make new friends! You just have to help me find the right place to do it. Maybe we can join a group together. Is there a Bible Study that we can join together? Is there a knitting club at the senior center that is appropriate for me? Sign me up. Go with me and enjoy it too.

Or maybe you need a break and a time to

reconnect with your own friends. Find a safe place for me to make new friends. Find an Adult Day Program where I can go and be social for a few hours every week. I may surprise you and want to go often. I can make friends, even if I don't remember their names or exactly what we do.

If I'm too afraid to be in a group of people, maybe you can find someone to come in to the house and visit with me. Don't tell me that they are my babysitter or caregiver – I certainly don't need that! (Or so I think). But bring in a friend to visit with me, and I may just have a great time while you go out and do what you need to do.

LET ME FEEL NEEDED

I do not want to be useless. I have spent my whole life helping other people, being useful, making things happen. Let me feel that again.

Maybe I can help you with some of the chores. Are there towels to be folded? Shirts to be ironed? I could set the table for you (who really cares where the knives and forks go, as long as you can find them when you want to eat!)

I can still rinse the dishes. Keep a watchful eye so I don't put dirty dishes back in the cupboard, but don't belittle me if I do. Go behind me later and make it right. Let me try to help if I want to.

OK, maybe I don't do the chores as efficiently as I used to. Maybe I don't even do them correctly anymore. But is there harm in letting me spend time doing them and feeling useful? You can always fix them when I've gone to bed tonight. Or you can simply throw away those "cookies" I made for you (after I've gone to sleep, of course.) I will feel so good to have contributed to the household, as I know everyone must.

You know I used to be a teacher. Let me do that again. Is there a small child that might enjoy going through a story book with me? Let me do that!

I can probably still feed the dog or take him for a walk. If I won't be able to find my way home, go with us. The walk will do us all good. Let me hold the leash if I can handle it. I'll feel good about it.

Maybe I can teach you or one of the kids something that I still do well. If I can still knit, let me show you how I do it. I won't be able to explain it completely, but you can always find a video or book and learn a little on your own, right?

ASK MY OPINION

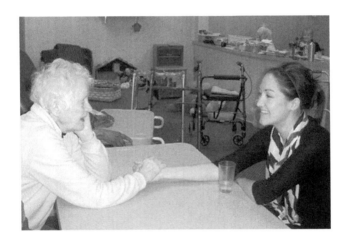

You used to ask me what I thought about things. I used to give you good advice. I may surprise you and give you good advice today.

If you are working through a problem, tell me about it. Ask me what you should do. I will feel like my opinion still matters. My answer may make sense. Or it may not. Does that matter? You were going to figure it out yourself anyway. But ask me what I think. Share the moment with me and see what happens.

When it's time to get dressed in the morning, don't just put out the clothes you want me to wear, ask me whether I'd like to wear the blue outfit or the pink. I probably have a preference. I'll gladly tell you, too!

Let's plan a trip together. Pull out those magazines or picture books and let's talk about it. How much time should we spend in Italy this time around? Oh, isn't that beach picture beautiful? Remember when we took that hike and got lost for 2 hours? Going through the photos and planning is half the fun of traveling, right? We can still do that, even if we can't actually leave our house anymore. Let's decide where we'll go together.

EXERCISE WITH ME

If my body is still healthy, let's take a walk. Take me as far as we can go. Take me to the garden center, and let's walk through the aisles and enjoy the plants. Take me to the beach and we'll walk along the shore. Let's go to the park and take that trail we love so much.

Take me swimming if we used to enjoy that. The local pool probably has a special class or time when we can enjoy the pool together.

Let's try yoga or Tai Chi together. Let's stretch and breathe and be healthy together. Maybe we can go to a senior center where they have special exercise classes. Let's find a DVD of walking exercises and do them along with the lovely lady on the TV. If you sit in front of me and do the exercises, I will likely imitate you. So let's do it together.

Moving my body will help keep me strong. Exercise releases stress. So let's do it!

WALK WITH ME

I may walk a little more slowly than I used to. I may have a bit of trouble with balance. I probably get lost if I walk alone. But I would still enjoy taking a stroll with you.

If I'm still steady on my feet and energetic, walking with you around the neighborhood or at a nearby park would be lovely. If distances are tough for me now, maybe we can take a drive to a garden center, and then stroll through the aisles there; enjoying the flowers…walking slowly here is most appropriate!

Walking in a mall might be enjoyable too…but please plan a day and time that it's not too crowded. Maybe we can go first thing in the morning, just as the shops are opening. We can do a little window shopping, then sit and enjoy a cup of coffee and watch the people walking by for a few minutes. That would be a great way to start a day with you.

I might even enjoy a stroll through a museum. That is usually a quiet place, and it certainly has a lot to see. I would love to look at the things there, and reminisce about the days gone by.

Did I used to enjoy a specific hobby? Let's head to the hobby shop on a quiet afternoon. As I walk in the door, the familiar sights and smells will no doubt give me a happy feeling.

Was I a seamstress in my younger years? A fabric store is a wonderful place to spend time walking and touching and remembering.

And maybe just a walk around the garden would be nice. Really I'd just like to spend a little time with you, arm-in-arm. Let's take a walk.

LET'S PLAY TOGETHER

I used to be so good at lawn games. I could beat anyone at croquet. I may surprise you and beat you again today.

Did you know I used to be a bowler? Get out that lawn bowling game, and let's play a set or two in the family room. The kids will enjoy it with us. We'll cheer each other on, we'll laugh and we'll have a blast.

Blow up a balloon, and let's try to keep it in the air. I don't know why that's fun…but it always is!

Bocce ball (the soft sets) is so fun. I don't even have to get out of my chair to play it (OK, someone has to pick up the balls and pass them out between rounds…but that can be you, right?) I can enjoy being successful whenever I roll that ball to the right place…you will be surprised how often I can do it!

Yes, I can toss a bean bag at a target on the floor. And I can enjoy doing it. I may say no if you ask me to do it. But set it up, and take turns playing too. We'll both be laughing and cheering in no time. Let's have some fun playing together.

DEAL THOSE CARDS

There are so many card games and board games that can be fun. I may not be able to play poker anymore, but how do you know if you don't try? I may surprise you.

If I can't follow the rules exactly, we can

change them. We can ignore them. We can use different rules whenever we play if we want to…who's to tell? We can play "cards up" so you can help me at my turn.

You can play solitaire as a team, did you know that? Set up the game and ask me to sit with you. I may be able to show you where to put the card…or I may just enjoy watching you do it.

There are a lot of family card games that are appropriate to play with me. Uno can be a lot of fun. You may want to throw out the cards that reverse the flow, as they confuse me. And some days you might want to ignore the cards that make me draw extras (some days that might make me upset). But I can probably still match numbers and colors. You might need to gently remind me what I can play. When you help me, do it with gusto. "Yeah, you have lots of yellow cards to choose from!" is so much better than "Look, it's easy. Just put down a yellow card." Remember, our goal is to have fun playing cards!

I may still be able to play poker or 21. Give it a try. Bridge and Canasta may be too hard for me now, but they are worth a try if I used to be a champ. With a supportive partner, I may still be able to play along.

Just be at the table with me. Let's keep our hands and our minds busy, and enjoy each others' company. That's what cards and games are for, remember?

LET'S CRAFT TOGETHER

You can find millions of craft ideas. Some are kits with all of the pieces. Some are simple supplies made into treasures. Find them at the craft store or the Dollar Store or in a catalog. Find ideas on Pinterest or in a magazine. Choose simple craft ideas (meant for kids or the untalented adults amongst us), and get the supplies.

Let's sit together and create something. It doesn't really matter what the end product looks like. The simple act of sitting together and using our hands and our creativity to put something together is what I will enjoy.

Maybe I'll join right in and make a perfect felt bird for the Christmas tree. Or maybe I'll sort the beads and baubles while you create something amazing. I can sort the flowers and ribbons while you create that perfect centerpiece for the party. If I'm at the table with you, and my hands are busy, I'm happy.

Hand me a paint brush and paper and see what I can do. It may be beautiful. It may be odd. But the act of creating it will likely make me happy today.

Do we have some coloring books? Not the children's books, but some adult books with nature scenes or intricate designs? Those could keep me busy for hours. I may imagine that I'm working...perhaps drafting again or working with blueprints. Maybe I used to draw beautifully, and now coloring in the designs is enjoyable. Does it matter what's going on in my head as long as I'm enjoying the process?

Give me a thread and needle, and show me how to make that little stuffed animal. Bring on the glue and the beads and the yarn. Let's make something wonderful together!

I'd love to work on a scrapbook with you. We can enjoy sorting the photos together...I will enjoy looking at each and every one. I may just watch you actually put the pages together. And you can bet that this scrapbook will take longer to create than any other you've done...but I'll enjoy every minute of it.

Buy me a paint-by-number set. I may be able to follow that exactly as it is intended...or I may just paint with the colors I want to. Either way, I'll enjoy it.

Let's make some cards together. We'll enjoy the creative process...even if we just do them from a kit. Then we can enjoy the writing and sending them. Great, right?

I can enjoy beading. If I don't have the dexterity to do small beads, buy larger beads Buy some pipe cleaners, and then let me put those beads on. I can create a great bracelet from this. Or I can just bead and un-bead it over and over. I'll enjoy feeling the beads and seeing the colors come together.

I may proudly display my handiwork afterwards. Or I may completely forget that I made that thing. Doesn't matter. The time we spent sitting together, working together, talking together…that's what matters.

HELP ME SEW AGAIN

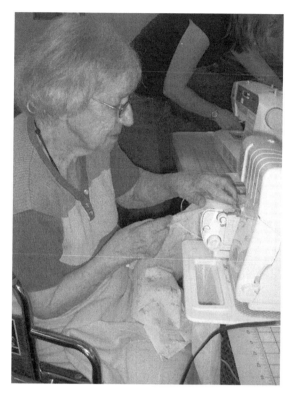

I used to love to sew. Help me do it again. Get out the sewing machine, find something easy for us to make, and let's get started. I can probably still cut something from a pattern. You may have to pin it, and you may need to fix it a little…but let's try and see.

When it's time to sew the seams, put me in front of the machine. Line up the fabric, watch me put my hands and feet in place, and see if I can't sew that baby up! Muscle memory will like take over, and my movements will be natural. You'll need to sit beside me and help me guide the fabric if I can't see so well anymore, or if my hands don't do exactly what I tell them to. But, hey, sitting next to you and doing this together is half of the fun!

When the seams are sewn, help me with the

finishing touches. Let me do whatever I can, just be there to help with the details that I can't handle anymore. The directions may be something I can no longer follow, but if you guide each step, I can still create something beautiful and/or useful.

There are tons of preprinted items in the sewing stores. If there is a new baby coming, maybe we can put together a little blanket or soft book. We could make bibs or burp cloths. Help me sew them. Help me wrap them up. Let me experience the joy of creating a gift for someone, and let them experience the joy of receiving something handmade by someone they love.

Even if we don't have a sewing machine available, I might be able to still do a simple cross-stitch project. Surely we can do a fringed fleece blanket together? That's just simple cuts and knots. I used to love to sew. Help me do it again.

LET'S PLAY DOMINOES

Dominoes sets can be found everywhere. Basic sets with up to 6 dots are very easy for almost anyone to play. I may be able to play with a larger set, though. That's more challenging, and you'll likely enjoy it more with me. Buy a large tin of dominoes, and let's give it a try!

If I can't figure out the moves myself, let's play with our tiles facing up. That way you can make suggestions if I get stuck. "Oh, how lucky! You have a six to play here" is a great way to make a suggestion without embarrassing me. Help me draw new tiles when I need to. Let me win once in awhile (but not always).

If we're playing with a group, be my partner. And when I can't do it anymore, let me enjoy stacking and sorting the tiles. They feel good in my hands. They feel familiar. They make me happy.

LET'S PLAY BOARD GAMES TOGETHER

I used to be the "Monopoly" champ. You know it. Maybe we can still play that game. But if not, there are lots of others.

"Sequence" is a good board game that just requires finding matches and making sets. I can probably still play that. If I don't understand it, we can be a team playing together with someone else.

Dice games are fun. Where is that "Yahtzee" game? I can still throw the dice (with gusto!) You can help me decide which to keep and which to throw again. We may get lucky!

BINGO is a great stand-by, and I may enjoy it. Change it up a little. Find a website that lets you create a new version with theme words. Let's make one for summer. Maybe you can make a set with pictures if I can't read anymore.

There is a great musical BINGO game where instead of numbers on the card, the song titles are listed. A CD with snippets of the songs is played, and while we play the game, we sing a few lines of the songs. Go back to that website and create cards with favorite Christmas songs or patriotic songs. Make a playlist on your iPod of those songs, and let's give it a whirl. We can sing a few lines or the whole song if we like it. The board game is really just an excuse to enjoy sitting and singing together in this case!

I can probably still play checkers pretty well. Dust off that board. How about

Backgammon? If I used to be able to play it, I might still be able to. What about Mancala? Moving the smooth stones around the board feels good, even if I don't remember the exact rules.

Find a "Blokus" game and let me make designs. We may not be able to play by the rules, but I will surely enjoy the feel of the tiles in my hands, I'll enjoy placing them, I'll enjoy the colors and the designs I create.

LET ME BAKE SOMETHING

I used to love making cookies for you. Remember? I would still like to do that.

Maybe I can't follow a recipe anymore. So read it for me. Gather the supplies. You do the hard parts...open the packages, do the measuring. Let me do the fun parts. I can still stir the ingredients (don't be surprised when I take a taste...that's how I know if it's good!)

This could be a great time to involve the

children. Who doesn't love mixing a batch of cookies and smelling them bake? Keep me safe, but let me do as much as I can.

If we're making an apple pie, I can probably still peel the apples. I'm not a child, and if I've held that knife and peeled apples for 70 years, I can probably still do it just fine. Keep an eye on me, but let me do what I can.

Use a timer so we remember when to take the cookies out of the oven. Heck, I needed a timer back when I could remember things! When they are ready, sit down and enjoy a cookie (or 2) and a glass of milk with me. Just like the old days.

LET ME HELP DECORATE

Is it Springtime and the daffodils are blooming? I may be able to make a beautiful bouquet for the table.

Remember when I decorated for every holiday (St Patrick's Day, Easter, 4th of July)? Let's do it again! Maybe we'll just have special items on the coffee table for each season...but what fun to put them out. I'll reward you by complimenting them every single day until it's time to change them. I promise.

Is it October? Let's make a jack-o-lantern together. I may be able to draw the face on the pumpkin. You can do the cutting, but let me help with cleaning out the inside. Maybe we can even roast those seeds like we used to!

Time for the Christmas tree? Yeah! Let's open the boxes and enjoy looking together at each ornament. Let me put some of them on the tree…as many as I'd like. When I get tired, let me sit and watch you finish the job. If the music is on, and we're chatting and remembering, how lovely is this evening?

I LOVE A GOOD PUZZLE

If my eyesight is failing or my fingers are fumbling, don't get crazy with the 1000 piece puzzles! But a good large size puzzle (300 pieces or less) can be put together in a few hours. Maybe we'll do it in one long afternoon, maybe we'll do a little each day for a month. But let's do it!

Choose beautiful pictures. As my abilities lessen, you can always find puzzles with larger, fewer pieces. I'll still enjoy working them with you.

If matching the pieces becomes too difficult for me, I may enjoy sitting at the table while you work on the puzzle. I'll enjoy the visiting we do while you work, and you'll have something to keep your mind and fingers busy while you talk to me. And, hey, ask me to find you that crazy piece with the blue edge…I can probably help you that way.

When I get to a point where I'm just lining up the pieces assigned to me, and I'm not helping with the piecing together, does that matter? As long as we're sitting together, doing something with our hands, isn't that OK?

WORD GAMES ARE AWESOME

If my memory is only just beginning to fail, I may be able to do a cross-word puzzle. As I start to forget, you may need to help me remember words, but we can do the puzzle together.

A good word search game is timeless. Even if my memory is bad, I can probably find words in the maze. I may circle them, I may cross them out. I will probably ask you more than once if the words can be diagonal too. But this may keep me busy while you get dinner. And after we eat, maybe we can do it together?

I've always enjoyed "Scrabble". I can probably still spell lots of words. Find a set with raised rails if my hands are shaky. Work with me as a team, and let's see how many words we can make together.

"Scattergories" is fun. We can do an easy version of it. Write five categories along the side of a sheet of paper – Food, Dessert, Famous People, Animals, and Places. Next choose a letter, and let's think of words starting with that letter to fit those categories. This is a great game to play as a group. Maybe the kids would like to join us.

I CAN STILL BUILD THINGS

OK, it may not be wise to give me a power saw and wood. But how about a "LEGO" set? Do you remember the "Lincoln Logs" you loved as a child? Remember who helped you build that cabin? I can still do that.

Get out that "Jenga" game, and see how well we can do as a team.

I used to be so good at building things. Maybe I can help put that model together. Maybe you'll need to sit with me and our grandchild while we do that...you may even need to do most of the work. If I feel like I'm helping, and our grandchild gets our undivided attention for the hour, isn't it all worthwhile?

Need something sanded? Tape some sanding paper to a table, and hand me the blocks. I can still remember how to do that motion...and I'll love the feel of the wood in my hand as it gets smoother and smoother.

Need to put together that shelf? OK, this may not work...but who knows? Let me help you. I can steady the pieces while you do the work. I will surely feel accomplished when it's done if I've had a hand in it.

Let me build something again.

SHARE YOUR COMPUTER WITH ME

If you are computer-literate, you have a treasure trove at your fingertips.

When I am in the earliest stages of dementia, I may actually be able to use the computer with you. Help me get to a website of interest, and let me read through it and enjoy it.

Hand me your iPad, set up one of the great game apps there and let me enjoy playing. I'll love the bowling game. I may really enjoy some of the word games. Do a search of memory games, and find some to try.

Use YouTube and pull up videos and music that we can enjoy together. Did you know that we can find Ed Sullivan, Dean Martin, old TV shows, old movies, favorite comedians there?

Pull up Pandora, type in one of my favorite old songs, and we'll have music to enjoy for the whole afternoon.

Set up a Facebook account for me. Let the kids know about it. Whenever I say something funny or smart, post it on my profile. When you catch me looking especially adorable (and you know I do look adorable most days!), take a photo and post it. The kids from around the country will no doubt type in comments here, even if they don't write me letters…and you can read them to me. We'll all enjoy the contacts. And we can spend countless hours looking at photos of all those adorable grandchildren I have. Who can tire of that?

Let's go look at Pinterest together. Type in flowers and let's see all of the breathtaking images there. Type in adorable children or kittens, and we'll have hours of fun.

Of course you can use traditional email to send letters for me, and when they are answered by those children of ours, print them out and let me carry them around to enjoy over and over.

I used to really enjoy decorating. Let's go online and find decorating ideas for our dream house again.

I love a good soccer game. Find the World Cup online, and let's watch it together.

If I can still play "Scrabble", let's start a "Words with Friends" game with my granddaughter in Virginia. We'll both enjoy the daily contact.

Load up the iPad with apps for kids, and hand it to my grandchild. He and I can sit for hours together enjoying the interactions. He'll do all of the playing, I'll enjoy cuddling with him and admiring the beautiful colors.

Yes, your computer or iPad are probably the most useful and wonderful tools you have to connect with me. Use your imagination and let's have some fun!

SHARE A TV SHOW WITH ME

TV can be a wonderful outlet for us. Don't just turn it on and walk out of the room. Find something for us to watch together, sit down beside me and let's enjoy the hour.

Don't choose a crime drama…that may scare me. I'll enjoy most comedy shows…especially the half hour family shows with laugh tracks. I'll chuckle right along with the audience.

I'll love shows like "Dancing with the Stars" and singing competitions.

Variety and talk shows can be good. "The Ellen DeGeneres Show" is always upbeat and fun.

Stay away from the news shows, because I may not be able to distinguish what's on TV from what's in our house. That can make me nervous.

Oh, please, find me the old black and white comedy shows! You know there is a TV station somewhere on the lineup that specializes in these. Find it. Record some of our favorites. I'll enjoy them over and over. "I Love Lucy", "My Three Sons", "Dick Van Dyke", "Lassie"…the list is endless. Try to stick to comedies or musicals, as I will find those most enjoyable.

Find the History Channel or something

similar and let me enjoy a documentary about Railroads. The Animal Channel can provide lots of entertainment. And if I have always enjoyed sports, let's watch that basketball game together. I'll probably still enjoy it.

Sometimes you'll be able to use the TV as a way to keep me occupied while you do something else...but probably not for long. I'll enjoy it a lot more if you sit with me. Let's sip coffee and have breakfast while watching a favorite show. Let's enjoy an hour of entertainment before I go to bed. Be with me. Talk to me about the show. Laugh with me. We'll both enjoy the show more together.

I LOVE CHILDREN

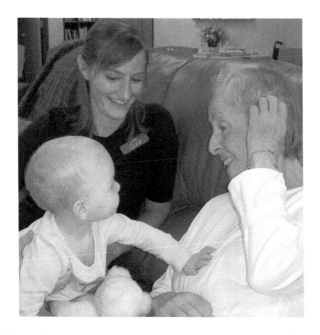

You don't want to leave me in charge of the little ones anymore...but I sure would enjoy seeing them!

If I loved being around your children in the past, I will love visiting with them still. I will probably call the grandchildren by my children's names...but it's only because I so fondly remember my time with my babies.

Keep us all safe. Stay right there with us as we visit. Help us to enjoy each other. Find something we have in common, maybe (we both love to sing, we both love to be read to). Or let the kids show off their new skills for me...I will love seeing them, they will love showing them...we'll all have fun.

Please remember, though, that lots of commotion and noise makes me anxious. A visit of a few minutes is probably enough for both of us. But, oh, those few moments are so wonderful!!

Bring the babies to me...I'd love to see them

TAKE ME TO LUNCH

OK, I know this can be tricky. Now that I have dementia, my manners may have slipped a little bit. The menu may be intimidating. I may forget that we've ordered, and be impatient with the waitress that I think has ignored us. I may lick the knife after I butter the biscuit. If those things bother you (or will bother others at a restaurant), let's not go there.

But we can still go to a small family restaurant can't we? Even a fast food restaurant where we can get french fries and coffee will be a treat to me.

Maybe we can go out for ice cream at the Dairy Queen? Nobody there will care that I lick the spoon...they are all doing it too!

Choose the time carefully. Let's go in the middle of the afternoon when it's not so busy and noisy...I'll have an easier time with it.

Guess what? Even when I have no manners left to sit in a restaurant, we can still get a treat at the drive-thru. Just being with you and enjoying a sweet treat or a hamburger is enough to make me happy.

REMINISCE WITH ME

Pull out those photo albums or local history books. Find the "Good Ol' Days" Magazine. Where are those old "National Geographic" and "Life" magazines? Pull them all out and have them at the ready.

Going through the pages, enjoying the images and the colors and the familiar faces will all bring me pleasure.

When we go through photo albums, you may be surprised at how much I remember. But if I don't remember things, help me. Point out the knick knacks in the background of the pictures that you remember fondly. Tell me the names of the babies. Remind me of how handsome my husband was. Laugh about that crazy pink lamp next to the chair.

Magazines that focus on the good old days are so fun to read. Go through them with me. Read the stories to me, share the photos, start the conversations. We'll both remember and learn something.

Photo-centric magazines like "National Geographic" or "Life" are wonderful conversation starters. Find them in the attic or in the second-hand stores, and keep a stack at the ready. They can help us remember things that have happened in our lifetimes. What a great thing to share with older children in the family. They will get a kick out of seeing odd fashions and old looking cars and toys…we'll enjoy sharing with them.

READ TO ME

Reading to someone is a true act of love. Think of how you enjoyed reading to your young children as you cuddled with them. Picture a romantic scene where a young man reads love poems to his betrothed. Think of the power of someone reading an inspirational story from the pulpit.

I may not be able to read a book anymore because I cannot see the words, or they don't make sense when I see them, or I just can't remember the storyline. But I will still enjoy listening to you read to me.

Choose books that are cute or funny. Short stories are best. "Readers Digest" with one paragraph stories and jokes are wonderful. "Chicken Soup for the Soul" books can be great (although be careful that you choose upbeat stories to read…stay away from the sad ones. I have enough sadness in my life.)

I'll even enjoy some of the children's classics. Dr Seuss's wonderful rhymes are entertaining. The sing-song of your voice will amuse me as you read them.

Read the newspaper to me (the headlines and the short story…don't bore me, for goodness sake!) Leave out the scary stuff. But tell me about the human interest stories. Read the scores for my favorite teams. I'm interested in what's happening in our city or in other places that I've visited. Share the stories and ask me what I think. Your acting like we can still have conversations may just help them to really happen every once in awhile. Won't that be nice?

Books with elaborate drawings are enjoyable to share. I'll enjoy as you read the story, and I'll enjoy getting lost in the pictures. Stories that involve small children or animals...especially those with lots of pictures...will always be winners for me. Poetry books are wonderful.

Read them to me after you've tucked me into bed. Just as that process relaxes children, it will relax me. Those quiet reading times will be times you'll treasure in your heart.

LET'S TELL STORIES

Share with me your favorite memories and stories from your childhood or youth. Share stories about your day or your family.

Ask me questions, and let me share my

stories. Sometimes I will repeat myself. Don't tell me you've already heard that story. Please listen to it again. Please laugh again, if it's funny. Act surprised by the outcome if that's appropriate. Act like it's the very first time you've heard this one.

If you want to keep things moving (and I know sometimes I will bore you), buy some books or conversation cards. Use them to help me remember new stories. Ask me different questions, and you may learn some new things about me. Or maybe everything I tell you is just made up. Who knows? Who cares?

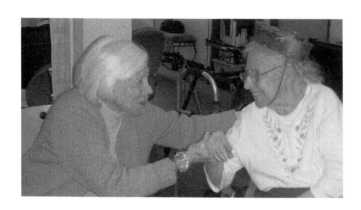

PLEASE CALL ME

Sometimes at the end of the day I get anxious. Even when I'm around people that I know, I start to worry that I need to get home. Maybe

I'm remembering wrong…I'm thinking that I need to get home to feed the kids. Whatever. I'm anxious.

Guess what can take that uneasy feeling away? A call from you! Hearing your friendly voice can transport me to a new, happier place. Let's chat about the weather. Tell me how your day went. Ask me about my day.

Now don't expect that our conversation will necessarily be about today. I may be remembering a day long ago. But let me tell you about it. And don't worry too much if I tell you things aren't going well. Please just reassure me.

Tell me that you love me. Tell me a joke. Tease me. Then tell me you love me again, and that you'll call again tomorrow.

If you live far from me, this is one thing that you can do for me every day. I'll love it.

CELEBRATE WHO I AM TODAY

This disease has changed me. I don't always act like the person you used to know. Sometimes what I do may embarrass you.

Our relationship has changed. I used to take care of you. I used to be able to truly contribute. Now it's difficult. What I used to do for you, you now have to do for me. That probably feels awkward to you.

I may not be able to show you that I appreciate what you are doing for me. I may not even realize that you are doing things for me. And I might even resent it when you make decisions for me.

But I still need you. I still need to know that you love me and that you appreciate me for who I am and for whom I once was. Please do not dwell on what is lost. Appreciate what we still have and help me enjoy this time that I have left.

TOUCH AND COMFORT ME

As my dementia progresses, my opportunities to touch others diminish. People don't trust me to hold small children. There are fewer and fewer people around me that actually touch me.

Humans need to be touched physically. To stay emotionally healthy, I need to feel close to you. When we walk together or sit together, hold my hand. Let's walk arm in arm. If I am also off balance, this kind of touch will keep me happy *and* safe.

When you walk past me, touch my shoulder. Rub my neck or my back if I enjoy that. A hand massage can work miracles. Show me that you still love me.

PRAY WITH ME

If I have been a faithful person in my life, my faith still matters to me. But I have probably lost my ability to worship and pray effectively. Help me to do that.

Maybe I can accompany you to worship services. Until late in my dementia, I can usually hold it together long enough to enjoy an hour long service. I will especially enjoy the music. I may enjoy the sermon or the prayers that are familiar to me.

Don't sit me in the middle of a large group of

people if you're worried that I might act out. Sit with me somewhere that allows us to leave quickly if need be. Then relax and enjoy the worship service with me. Help me to sing the hymns. Hold my hand during the service. Help me to partake in communion if that's appropriate.

At home, as in church, it is important to pray. Help me to do that. Keep your worries about me as quiet prayer between you and God. When you pray with me, let's bless the people we love. Use formal prayers and Bible verses that are familiar to me. Help me keep my faith alive. Pray with me.

FINAL THOUGHTS

We hope that you have found a few ideas that you can use in your daily life. Being a family caregiver is a long and difficult journey. Take time to enjoy the small things.

The ideas we've presented here can be enjoyed one-on-one, and in groups. Some are very appropriate for including children. Some of these ideas should be used every single day (touch and prayer, for instance.)

Others can be saved for special occasions.

Try not to do everything yourself. Just because your loved one will enjoy crafts or playing cards doesn't mean you will. Maybe that's a perfect idea for your son to use while he takes a turn caring for Dad so you can have a break. Maybe you can find an Adult Day Program in your area that offers many of these activities so your loved one can have some fun and you can have some rest. Maybe you'll hire an in-home caregiver to help you, and you can provide them with a list of favorite activities.

Remember to forgive yourself when you can't find the fun in the moment. We're all just human beings trying to make it through. You're facing some special circumstances that make life challenging. Make it your goal to have some fun with the person you love every single day. If today it doesn't work…sleep on it and try again tomorrow. You'll both be happier for it.

God bless you on your journey.

ABOUT THE AUTHOR

Marcie M. Jones is the co-founder of Gentog, LLC, an intergenerational daycare program located in Tigard, OR. Marcie had the privilege of being one of the primary caregivers for two years for her Grandma Helen, who is featured in several of the photos in this book. Helen was a daily participant in the Gentog program for those 2 years, and continues to visit regularly. When someone read the first draft of this book, she commented, "I could hear your feisty little grandma talking as I was reading." Indeed, many of the scenarios here were created from Marcie's experience in caring for her Gram.

Major contributors to the Gentog Adult Day Program and to the ideas within this book are Cathy Ranck and Lisa Rice. They have been with Gentog since our beginning. As our Personal Care and Activities Directors, they have truly been the heart and soul of the Gentog Senior Program. Cathy and Lisa are constantly on the look-out for ideas for new activities and experiences for our seniors. Everything contained in this book has been tried successfully in our program.

You can learn more about Gentog on our website at www.gentog.com.

Like us on Facebook at www.facebook.com/generationstogether.

Follow us on Pinterest at www.pinterest.com/gentogllc.

Or visit us in person! You can find us at

11535 SW Durham Rd #C5
Tigard, OR 97224
503-639-2600

5652636R00051

Made in the USA
San Bernardino, CA
15 November 2013